NIAGARA FALLS

Irving Weisdorf & Co., Ltd.

*Niagara River tumbles over the **Rainbow Falls** into its new home.*

Niagara Falls, a natural wonder of beauty and majesty, has thrilled and inspired aesthetics, thrill seekers and lovers since man first beheld it. For thousands of years this superb spectacle was known only to Native Peoples. Portaging on their journeys, they heard the roar long before they actually saw the Falls. It sounded like continual thunder so they named it **Onguiaahra** (later Niagara) which means "Great Thunderer of Waters." Dazzled by its beauty and power, successive tribes, claimed the Falls as their own. For all Natives, the Falls carried spiritual significance for a powerful, demanding god dwelt in the cataract.

Historians report that the first European to view the Falls was **Father Louis Hennepin**, a French priest who accompanied the explorer LaSalle. His first impressions must have been awe but his writings show dread, as they read *"These waters foam and boil in a fearful manner. They thunder continually."* Seems a limited assessment for a prie adventurer. However, the Falls he witnessed carrie more than twice the volume of water we see now.

Today, hydro-electric production diverts close to two thirds of the Falls' flow to keep Ontario an Eastern U.S.A. warm, bright, and functioning. Overawed now, just imagine what we might see!

*The **Horseshoe Falls** in all its power and magnetism*

*Rainbow Falls with **Maid of the Mist** in foreground - Crowds of spectators line the escarpment at **Luna Island**.*

THEY COME FOR THE VIEW

And they find it everywhere. On your initial visit you'll probably join throngs of spectators along the sidewalk at the brink of the precipice. From here you can stand directly opposite the lovely **American Falls**, two Falls actually, the main or **Rainbow Falls** and the dainty **Bridal Veil**, separated by **Luna Island**. Stroll southward toward the Canadian or **Horseshoe Falls** which carries 90% of the flow. One look at this tremendous cataract will literally take your breath away. At regular intervals along the walk powerful magnifying viewers afford close-up studies.

You might get wet from the spray, but that's part of the adventure. Some say you haven't been to the Falls unless you've felt the mist.

In literature the classic view of anything takes place from a bridge. So with Niagara the **Rainbow Bridge** offers an overall look at both Falls, the rapids, the **Maid-of-the-Mist** and, almost every day, a rainbow. More specialized views above, below, behind and beside are all attainable to enhance your already exciting impression.

*Visitors throng at the brink of **Horseshoe Falls** every day through the summer.*

◄ *The imposing **Skylon Tower** captures the whole Niagara scene.*

*Rainbows make the **Horseshoe Falls** even more breathtaking and make wonderful photo opportunities.*

*Helicopter view of both the **American Falls** and the **Horseshoe Falls** with the **Rainbow Bridge** in the forefront.*

While taking in the wonderful view helicopter passengers enjoy an exciting ride.

◄ *One of North America's largest casinos and a must-see attraction.*

For a bird's eye view and a fabulous photographing opportunity, nothing surpasses a helicopter ride, available from one of three aerial tour companies, any day of the year, subject to weather conditions.

An elevator ride through solid rock carries you down to **Table Rock Scenic Tunnels** where you may walk through corridors behind **Horseshoe Falls**. Through open windows in these tunnels you get a splendid look at the waterfall as it plummets in front of you. Another tunnel takes you to an outdoor observation platform where you stand almost level with the Falls. History books show pictures of early explorers hoisting the flag of France at approximately this same spot. *And they had to get there on foot!*

A favorite viewpoint, dating back to 1846, is the **Maid-of-the-Mist** boat tour through the turbulent waters and rocky channels at the base of both Falls.

Niagara Falls N.Y. from the air. Great View of **Goat Island** and it's companions. **Convention Center** in distance.

*The **Minolta Tower** is easily accessible via the comfortable incline railway. Passengers can enjoy a spectacular view of the falls while reaching the top of the escarpment.*

The Observation Platform on the American side will elevate you far above the river to an outdoor platform for an aerial view. More exciting is when the same elevator takes you down to the rocky ledges directly beside the **American Falls**. This attraction is open year round but on a bright winter day it's an amazing thrill to stand on the ledge and actually watch the mist freezing. Take your camera as this natural display, formed at the whim of wind and temperature, is never the same twice.

◄ *Observation Platform from which people can walk close to the cataract or ascend to viewing area.*

*Victoria Park Restaurants and gift shops.
Skylon Tower in background.*

*Evening at Skylon Tower,
shops and games below dinner and entertainment above.* ➤

A comfortable sit-down view can be had from any of the fine restaurants in the park area. Closest to the Falls is **Table Rock Restaurant** where you still feel in contact with the boiling waters. Multi-windowed dining rooms of **Victoria Park Restaurant** and **The Skyline Foxhead** also offer excellent views. For a panoramic vista of the Falls and surroundings, take your dinner at one of Niagara's imposing towers. The Minolta's **Top of the Rainbow** is a four-time winner of the prestigious Restaurant of the Year award. **Skylon Tower's** revolving dining room gives not only a view of the Falls but an interesting study of the business and architecture of this bustling border city. Both towers house exhibits, gift shops and recreational areas.

Interior of Skylon dining room. When you stop to eat you keep the Falls in view.

*A spectacular fountain lights up the night in **Queen Victoria Park**.*

PARKLANDS

The early nineteenth century witnessed an influx of sightseers from far and near. They camped along the shore, bought provisions from farmers and enterprising dealers. And so the hospitality industry began. Opportunists and entrepreneurs eyed this growing market and flocked to take advantage of it. They crowded into prime areas hawking shoddy souvenirs and doubtful services. Concern that the beauty of the site would be destroyed by this infiltration, the governments on both sides of the border sought to secure the lands adjacent to the Falls for permanent parkland.

The Canadian side was later to increase its authority to include a stretch of land the entire length of the **Niagara River**. Maintenance and development are now controlled by **The Niagara Parks Commission**. Picnic grounds, walking, biking, and wheelchair trails, a golf course, information and refreshment facilities are among the amenities along the Parkway.

Horseshoe Falls in full color.

Rainbow (American Falls) in glowing white.

*Rose Garden and fountain in **Niagara Falls Greenhouse** area. **Minolta** and **Skylon Towers** look on from the background.*

The **formal gardens** and **Oakes Theatre** are favorite spots for lovers and dreamers. To the immediate south is **Queen Victoria Park**, great for family gatherings and leisurely walks any time of year. There you'll come upon **Niagara Falls Greenhouse** with extravagant displays for every season. Open every day but Dec. 24 & 25. Just beyond the greenhouse is the ever popular **Marineland**, a famous and favorite show and play park.

Things quiet down when you reach **Dufferin Islands**, south of the **Horseshoe Falls**. Considering its surroundings, this natural woodland is unbelievably tranquil. Here in the backwaters of the violent upper river, you may safely swim, wade, or ride paddle boats. Especially lovely in autumn. Interestingly you're likely to meet as many locals as tourists here.

*Children paddle boating around peaceful **Dufferin Island**.*

***Niagara Botanical Gardens,** a feast for the eyes and nose.*

Going north along the Niagara Parkway, past the lower rapids and whirlpool, you approach **Niagara School of Horticulture** and **Niagara Parks Botanical Gardens**. Lose yourself in this one hundred acres of flowering plants, herbs, trees, and shrubs. Farther north you come to **Niagara's famous floral clock**, formed of 15,000 plants. Next to the clock is the lilac garden where 1500 varieties of lilacs will delight your eyes and nose each May.

The Niagara Glen, across from the School of Horticulture provides one of the region's most exciting walks. A trained guide will lead you down the gorge to the very edge of the river. The **Queenston-Lewiston Bridge** is the site geologists estimate to be the birthplace of Niagara Falls. The continuous process of erosion has driven this phenomenon to its present position.

Autumn is a wonderful time of year to see the beauty of the parks in and around **Niagara Falls**.

Springtime brings new colour to the region.

*The **Brock Monument** in Queenston Heights Park.*

Picnic pavilions, recreation facilities and free Sunday concerts make **Queenston Heights Park** an oasis for visitors as well as Niagara residents. The imposing monument to **Sir Isaac Brock** who gave his life in the struggle to keep this part of Canada for Canadians, dominates the skyline high above the park and river. Those intrepid souls who brave the 235 spiralling steps to the top get to feast their eyes on one of the grandest views in the world. Nature is on display here from woodlands and vineyards to sailboats and steamers, the Falls, the rapids, the top of Toronto, and everything between.

No description of Niagara's parks would be complete without reference to **Goat Island** and its companions on the American side of the river. These lands are by State mandate less developed than their counterparts in Canada, which makes the island ideal for nature study and romantic or invigorating walks. There's still plenty of forest and natural woodland. Regular spray from the Falls enhances the atmosphere for growth of trees, shrubs, and wildflowers. Although the perspective on the Falls is limited, the proximity of the mighty upper rapids, the spray, and the ever-present roar sanctify this lovely island.

***Goat Island** separates the American Falls from the Horseshoe Falls and offers a unique vantage point to experience the rapids.*

*The lower **Niagara River** near Queenston is a safe haven for boaters of all types.*

*The autumn colours offer a strong contrast to the grassy areas of **Niagara Parks.***

*The remarkable **Jean Francais Gramlet (Blondin)** is still regarded as Niagara's favorite daredevil.*

Bobby Leach and his barrel.

DAREDEVILS

As you do the rounds of Niagara Falls you will see and hear frequent references to the daredevils who challenged the Falls or rapids. Some will state that this one or that one "conquered" Niagara. But really the men and women who performed these feats did it for adventure, not for war. To them the river was not a foe, but a playmate, daring them to join in a most exciting odyssey.

The most popular and memorable daredevil was a French tightrope walker, Jean Francois Gravalet, known as **Blondin**, who, in 1848 crossed the gorge on a tightrope. Blondin repeated his success not once but many times, performing unimaginable feats such as pushing a wheelbarrow, wrapped in a sack, and carrying his manager on his back. Most amazing was the time he carried a portable stove to the center where he stopped to light a fire and cook an omelet. He served this on china plates and lowered it to the Maid-of-the-Mist, far below. For a while Blondin was a greater attraction than the Falls. His unparalleled mastery of balance was almost matched by his keen sense of comedy and his love of an audience. Other skilled

Annie Taylor is helped to shore after a successful and harrowing journey.

tightrope artists followed, but none had the magic or charisma of Blondin. Maybe because he was first.

Those who went over the Falls in a barrel were excluded from contact with their audiences. Isolated in dark contraptions they braved the thundering cataract alone. The first successful such traveler was **Mrs. Annie Taylor,** a sixty-three-year-old school teacher from Bay City, Michigan. In the year 1901, Mrs. Taylor supervised the design and construction of her own barrel and declared confidently that she'd go over the Falls and live. To the amazement of skeptics and scoffers, this determined woman came through the adventure unharmed. Others followed in containers more or less scientifically designed. Only five survived.

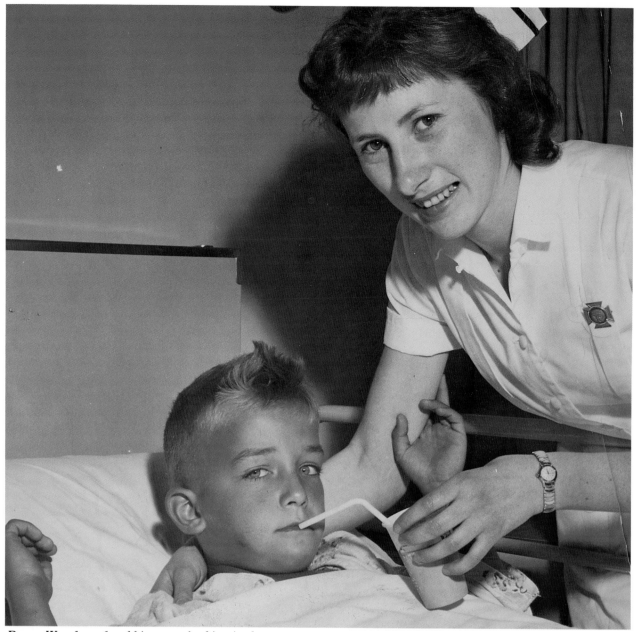

Roger Woodward and his nurse after his miracle rescue.

In the case of seven-year-old **Roger Woodward** there was no motivation. Victim of a boating accident on the upper river, Roger was carried over the Falls, protected by only a life jacket, and rescued by the Maid-of-the-Mist. When the captain, **Christopher Keech** declared him alive, a resounding cheer arose from both crew and passengers. Niagara Falls had delivered a miracle.

Meanwhile, near the brink of Horseshoe Falls, Roger's sister, **Deanne**, was thrashing about, some distance from shore when she was spotted by **John Hayes**, a tourist from New Jersey. Without a thought for himself, Mr. Hayes climbed over the guard rail at Terrapin Point. He heard the girl's weak cries and called "swim for your life, over this way." He reached out over the rushing water until Deanne was able to grasp his thumb. Hayes, in danger of being swept into the cascade, called for help. A second man, **John Quatrocchi** of Pennsylvania, climbed over the rail and helped complete the rescue. Although Deanne's ordeal was not as sensational as that of her brother, it's worth recounting that two men, absolute strangers to the girl and to each other, risked their lives to save a fellow human being. The angry river claimed both the boat and its owner-operator.

Dave Munday prays beside his barrel.

Once was not enough for stuntman John David Munday. Lured by danger this non-swimmer made his first attempt in July 1985. However, police notified Hydro authorities who reduced the flow and Munday was caught in a hydro basin above the Falls. Determination caused Munday to return with his barrel on Oct 5 of the same year and he made the plunge successfully.

In July 1990 Munday was foiled again when his barrel stuck on a rock at the brink of the Horseshoe. He didn't give up. On September 26 1993, 8 years after his first success, Munday became the first person ever to survive two barrel trips over Niagara Falls.

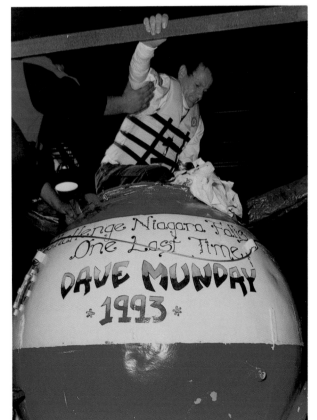

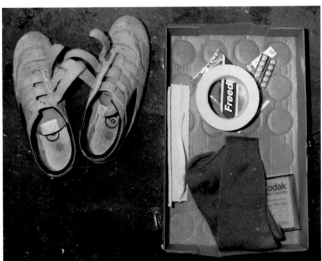

Munday's lucky charms.

Munday is rescued.

Previous page: **Dave Munday** *on September 26, 1993 survived his second barrel trip over the Falls*

Munday is helped out of his barrel alive and well.

Any account of the bold and brave has to include Niagara's own **William (Red) Hill**. This man's entire life revolved around Niagara River. Though he never attempted to go over the Falls he served those who did, braving the rapids to retrieve these adventurers and their sometimes broken and leaking crafts. Three times he rode the rapids from the **Whirlpool** to Queenston. He devoted his life to serving those in danger, counselling river acrobats, rescuing casualties, and recovering bodies of accident or suicide victims. Four times he was awarded the Humane Association's Medal for Bravery-the first when, as a boy of nine, he saved his sister from a burning house. Except for a period in the army during World War I, Red Hill lived all his life in Niagara Falls, regarding himself not as a stuntman or daredevil, but simply a riverman.

Daredevil memorabilia and newspaper reports can be seen at the museum or at Imax Theatre. Well worth investigating.

William Red Hill.

Imax Theater completely involves its audience in numerous spellbinding adventures. Imax is not a movie. It's an experience!

Niagara Falls Museum established in 1827, is the oldest museum in North America.

Amazing giant redwood tree from in **Humbolt County, California** *a favorite with museum visitors.*

*The **Museum** houses a far East exhibit including the oldest Egyptian mummy in existence.*

*The **Museum** houses an exhibit of oddities.*

DIVERSIONS AND ATTRACTIONS

For armchair adventure you won't find anything better than **IMAX Theater's** presentation **NIAGARA: MIRACLES, MYTHS, AND MAGIC.** Sit back in comfort, loosen your shoes and become involved.

Students as well as tourists appreciate a tour of **Niagara Falls Museum.** Established in 1827, it is the oldest museum in North America. Here you'll see some actual daredevil barrels as well as historical artifacts, pictures and writings from Niagara's early times. It is also a good general museum with near and far East exhibits including the oldest and best preserved **Egyptian mummy** in existence. Many visitors leave messages on the remains of the largest redwood tree ever felled. Located at 5651 River Road, the museum is open year round.

Marineland's killer whales endear themselves to their audience at every performance.

*Performing **sea lions** not only enjoy their audience but obviously appreciate one another.*

*The **deer** and **elk** have no fear. Neither have the children.*

Dolphins *display their skills.*

Besides its undisputed status as one of the world's most awesome and romantic spots, the Falls' area teems with places of amusement, excitement, and information. By far the most popular of these attractions is **Marineland**. Here people of all ages thrill to the antics of acrobatic sea lions, dolphins and regal killer whales. There's also a friendly deer and elk population which just loves to be petted. Children from one to a hundred may top off their stay with any of the thrilling Marineland rides. One admission covers everything.

Spanish Aero Car for those who crave the thrill of being part of the action.

The aforementioned **Maid of the Mist** cruise is a must, something everyone should do at least once. No cabins here, no dining room, no deck chairs. Nevertheless this is a pleasure cruise in the true sense of the word. Passengers in rainwear (supplied) are all in holiday mood. With three boats in operation the tours leave every fifteen minutes from both Canadian and American docks. A daytime adventure, May to October.

Great Gorge Adventure and **Spanish Aero Car**, both offer the Whirlpool experience, one by elevator and boardwalk, the second by cable car swinging right above the seething whirlpool.

Passengers.

Signs of erosion. Fallen rocks change forever the pattern of the river's flow.

*View of rapids showing **Spanish Aero Car.***

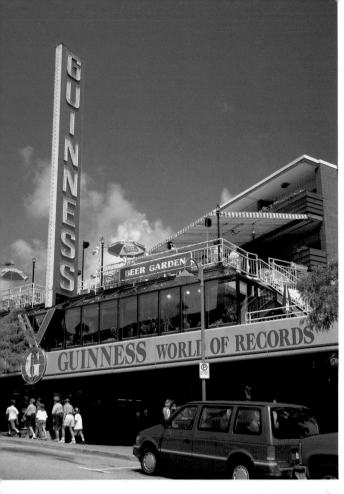

On a hot day just looking at water isn't always enough. You want to be there. In that case you'll enjoy **Whitewater Waterpark** where you can ride a twisting and turning water slide into a surf-wave pool. Smaller slides and pools for little ones make this an adventure for the whole family.

For laughs, surprises, and real horrors the place to go, and you can't miss it is **Clifton Hill**. Here you'll find high-pulse activity, fun houses, strange, comical, and horrifying museums, kiddie rides, shops and foods. This vibrant street could be called Niagara's Laugh-In. Everybody, absolutely everybody, who visits Niagara spends some time on Clifton Hill. And that's twelve million souls a year. Niagara residents also come, just for the fun of it.

*Not only beautiful, **Niagara Falls** is lots of fun too.*

Visiting the Falls is great, but why not also EXPERIENCE them? You can do just that with **Ride Niagara**, "The Ultimate Thrill" an exciting new adventure! This award-winning attraction is fun and entertainment for all ages. Enjoy your own "personal journey" over Niagara Falls in the safety of an amazing, computerized motion simulator.

Everyone loves to see a butterfly, so how about seeing at least 2,000 in one day? You can do this with a visit to the new **Niagara Parks Butterfly Conservatory**. This year round exhibit will be home to a wide variety of butterflies from around the world, complete with nectar producing flowers and a lush, rain forest environment.

In total comfort and safety, the reliable Drax E-1000 allows you to challenge thundering Niagara on **Ride Niagara** *- the ultimate thrill.*

This **Viceroy Butterfly** *(Basilarchia Archippus) is one of 2,000 to see at the* **Niagara Parks Butterfly Conservatory***.*

People Mover transports passengers to all points of interest.

Double decker bus, a favorite guided tour.

GETTING AROUND

Holidays can be hard on a driver. Niagara Parks has come up with a viable solution—its own **People Mover**. Operating through the busy season this service extends from Rapids View Parking Lot south of Dufferin Island to the Spanish Aero Car, from the first of May to mid-October, and to Queenston Heights Park mid-June to Labour Day. The movers run at fifteen minute intervals and your inexpensive pass is good all day. You can get on and off as often as you like. First time visitors might like a more structured tour of Niagara's attractions. For them there are regular tour buses (red double-deckers are a favorite.) They take in the main sights and deliver historical and geological facts as they go.

Queen Street Niagara-on-the-Lake.

IT DOESN'T END HERE

Nobody said it better than the late great **Sir Winston Churchill** who called Niagara Parkway "The prettiest Sunday drive in the world." This from a man who'd been practically everywhere. So try to take in the drive to **Niagara-on-the-Lake** at the mouth of the river. This lovely town, the first Capital of Upper Canada, has its own unique culture and charm. The citizens strive to maintain the nineteenth century flavor of the town and most buildings reflect this. No honky-tonk here and no golden mile. Big emporiums, vapid malls, and cheap souvenir vendors are not tolerated. But friendly shopkeepers are happy to help you select fine china, jewelry, gifts and clothing. For children there's a downtown park with pool and playground which they may follow with a trip to an ice cream parlor or a homemade fudge shop.

St Andrew's Church, *a step back to early Canadian houses of worship.*

Mementos to **Laura Secord** *renowned for heroics. Her home is now a museum.*

The Living Water wayside chapel welcome

The Clock Tower and the Court House.

*Theatre is alive and well in **Niagara**.*

*The **Royal George Theatre** is also used during the Shaw Festival.*

Restored **Prince of Wales Hotel** caters to theater lovers and those who like a good time.

Festival Theatre has entertained royalty, diplomats and its constant mainstay - the general public.

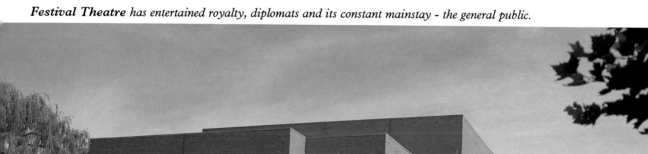

Shaw poster

*Roll out the barrel, **Niagara vintners** compete with the best in the world.*

Niagara's unique cool climate growing region produces quality grapes for award-winning wines.

For theatre lovers **Niagara-on-the-Lake** is home to the renowned **Shaw Festival**. This fine company of players offers the works of **G. B. Shaw** and his contemporaries on three stages, the only company in the world with such a commitment. It's a great advantage to get on the mailing list as the program is announced and tickets go on sale well in advance.

Niagara Region produces 80% of Canada's grapes and countless prize winning wines, and Niagara-on-the-Lake is surrounded by vineyards. Be sure to include a winery tour on your visit. Take a taste of a world-famous wine right from the vintner.

Niagara proudly provides one of the most picturesque wine routes in the world.

History buffs will enjoy a tour of historic **Fort George**, a strategic site during the War of 1812. Another point of interest, **Niagara Apothecary**, is really a museum of pharmacology. The town's churches are mainly nineteenth century buildings retaining their original character. Be sure to stop at the **Wayside Chapel**, on Niagara Parkway.

*Historic **Fort George**.*

*The **Maid of the Mist** tours close under the American Falls to the Horseshoe Falls.*

SAVE THE VISION

While sightseers and daredevils amused themselves, governments looked with concern toward the talus at the base of the American Falls. Though the water fell from a height of 182-184 ft., the talus of broken rock at the base was steadily rising, reducing the drop in some spots by a third and diminishing the beauty of the Falls. A corps of engineers and geologists was engaged to divert the American Falls to go over the Horseshoe so they could conduct a survey of the base to determine if part of the talus could be removed, and if future rockfalls could be prevented. The survey continued for five months at which time they concluded that Nature must take its course as removing the talus could precipitate a massive breakup of the cliff wall. The flow was reinstated and Niagara Falls returned to its natural state. Strangely, during the diversion, while a major portion of Niagara's attraction no longer appeared, there was a surge in tourism. A dry Niagara Falls, cluttered, derelict and stark naked was something worth seeing.

The **Rainbow Bridge** joins Canada to the United States and is lit up beautifully each night.

The parks and gardens along the **Niagara Parkway** are worth a stroll.

WHEN TO GO

Majesty has no off-season. For their own convenience and to take advantage of the attractions the majority of visitors come in summer. Most attractions continue through October, making autumn ideal for those who can make their own time. But the spectacle in winter is breathtaking. Snow, ice, wind, and spray create exquisite works of art, which differ year by year, day by day, even hour by hour.

Every so often a winter occurs that favors the formation of an **ice bridge**. An early deep freeze followed by a warming trend and sunlight are ideal conditions for this phenomenon. The longest-lasting ice bridge on record occurred in 1899, lasting from January 9 to April 11. Ice tumbled in giant hunks over the Falls to break up, float, refreeze and finally settle in a series of hills, gullies, and crevasses. As soon as word got out tourists poured in. People raced to be first to cross the bridge. For most it was the challenge of their lives.

*The **Minolta Tower** is decorated for the Festival of Lights and Christmas every year.*

*Historic **Ice Bridge** helped tourists get a unique view of the Falls.*

*Winter is an enchanting time to visit **Niagara Falls** day or night the scenery is breathtaking.*

The ice bridge with a bonus took place in 1938. Bridge authorities were already concerned about the strength of the **Steel Arch Suspension Bridge,** the main crossing between the two cities. They watched the weather vigilantly and when ice from Lake Erie flowed down the river in January they immediately closed the bridge. By late January the river was jammed with ice 18 m. (60 ft.) thick from Horseshoe Falls to Youngstown 26.4 km. (16.5 mi.) down river. Nature on the rampage has no respect for man-made structures and down came the busiest border crossing between Canada and U.S.A. Ten thousand spectators were on the scene within minutes, and they continued to pour in. People came by train, bus and car to see the ice bridge and its casualty, and to brave the frigid walk. In April that the last piece of bridge floated down river on a slab of ice. The new crossing, the **Rainbow Bridge,** officially opened in October 1941.

*Even in winter-**Rainbows** are never far away.*

In recent years winter has been celebrated at Niagara Falls with the enchanting **Festival of Lights** from mid-November to mid-January. Through the parks on both sides of the river, lighting displays, storyland tableaux and concerts delight both visitors and residents. Hours of illumination of the Falls are extended so no one can ignore the main event. Favorite spots are **Victoria Park** in Canada and the **Wintergarden** at Niagara Falls N.Y.

*Spring brings the **Blossom Festival** to Niagara Falls.*

Spring ushers in a fresh season and Niagara Falls and area gear up for the annual **Blossom Festival**. Streets and parks are a veritable fairyland resplendent with fruit trees in bloom as well as massive displays of lilacs and magnolias. From now on everything is in full swing. Welcome to **Niagara Falls**.

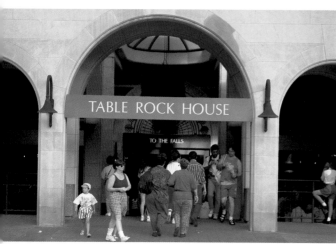

WHERE WERE YOU WHEN THE LIGHTS WENT OUT?

At 5.16 On November 9, 1965 a break in one of the Adam Beck generating plants on the Canadian side precipitated the greatest power failure in North American history. Thirty million people were thrust into utter blackness as Ontario, New York and the Eastern States came to a standstill. To all it was an inconvenience, to some it was a disaster. Coming as it did, right at rush hour, it caused havoc in big cities. In New York City thousands were trapped in crowded subways. Others spent hours on airless elevators, while still others remained high in office towers. Airline pilots preparing for landing looked down and saw absolutely nothing and felt rather as if they had flown into a vacuum or a black hole, or maybe the end of the world. Similar situations happened in other cities, like Toronto and Boston. But of course New York, being the biggest, suffered the most. Also for the longest—thirteen and one half hours.

Published and Distributed by

Irving Weisdorf & Co. Ltd.
2801 John Street,
Markham, Ontario L3R 2Y8

Text by
Joan Colgan Stortz

Designed by
David Villavera

Computer layout by
Amy Morrison

Photographer	Page
Thies Bogner, **Bogner Photography Ltd.**	7b, 9a
C. Cheong	8
G. Counsell	3, 22a, 22b, 23a, 23b, 52a, 53a, 53b, 54b, 55
John Daly, courtesy of **The Niagara Parks Commission**	42b
Festival of Lights	56a, 56b, 57a, 57b, 60g
L. Fisher	Front cover, Back cover, 1, 2, 4/5, 6, 7a, 9b, 10a, 10b, 11, 12a, 12b, 13, 14, 15a, 15b, 16/17, 18, 19a, 19b, 20/21, 24a, 24b, 25a, 26a, 33b, 34a, 35a, 38a, 38b, 39a, 39b, 40a, 40b, 40c, 41a, 41b, 41c, 41d, 41e, 41f, 43a, 43b, 44, 45a, 45b, 45c, 45d,46a, 46b, 46c, 47a, 47b, 48a, 48b, 49b, 50, 51a, 51b, 60a, 60b, 60c, 60d, 60e, 60f, 60h, 61a, 61b, 61c, 61d, 61e, 61f, 62/63
Marineland	36a, 36b, 37a, 37b
J. Neiss, Niagara Gazette©	29a, 29b, 29c, 30/31, 32a, 32b
Courtesy of the **Niagara Falls Museum Ltd.**	26b, 27, 33a, 34b, 35b, 52b
The Niagara Parks Commission	54a, 58a, 58b, 58c, 58d, 59
Courtesy of Ride Niagara	42a
R. Roels, courtesy of the **Niagara Falls Museum Ltd.**	28
R. W. Walker	48c
C. Wittmann	25b, 49a